THE TENTH MUSE

THE TENTH MUSE

Poems and Prose on the Arts

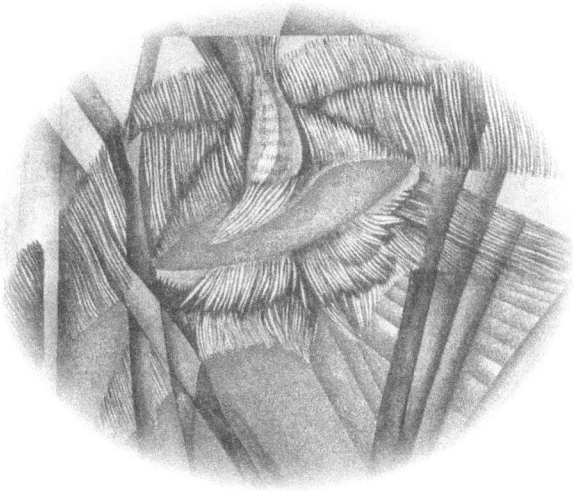

Leah Shelleda

ISBN 978-1-952194-11-5

Cover image original oil painting by Melanie Gendron

Design by River Sanctuary Graphic Arts

Printed in the United States of America

Additional copies available from:
www.riversanctuarypublishing.com
amazon.com

River Sanctuary Publishing
P.O Box 1561
Felton, CA 95018
www.riversanctuarypublishing.com
Dedicated to the awakening of the New Earth

For Bill

*The best love is the one that awakens our soul
and makes us reach for more*

The Tenth Muse

1
Tenth muse
are you the ultimate anonymous
the first erasure
When did it happen?
Was a muse for art   so dangerous
they had to get rid of you ?
Did they imagine a future
when the word image
became the word for god?

2
Was it the Olympians
who sent you into
exile
outsider   outlier   outlaw
I believe you kept your powers
how I do not know
   well I may
      but that's another story
Getting back to the gods
who sent you into exile -
a lot of good it did them

3
A muse must only inspire
Did you break the rule?
Did you pick up a chisel a brush
Can you believe the muse of lyric poetry never sang
Can you imagine Terpsichore the muse of dance
                                        unmoved

4

If there was no muse where does
the impulse to paint   to carve
come form
is it a warmwild woman
a souldance man
a hover of wingspan
a scene of such feeling…..
Is it
the greedy eye
looking outward
taking it all in?

5

But what if there was a muse
who didn't inspire art
but goodness?
What if she had a scheme –
Give them excellence
give them empathy
fill the heads and hearts
of those
with nimble hands
They would cast wisdom in bronze
carve truth on temple pediments
and she showed them the beautiful boys
with their perfect bodies and curly hair
she thought that love would lead
to the Good
She came to the city
where they only idealized power
She whispered the words *philo sophia*
into a poor teacher's ear
and fled

6

Calliope Enterpe Erato
muses of epic lyric & love
may I have a word with you?
Calliope
I don't write epics
warriors don't call to me
Erato
the only songs you bring me
must not be sung
Enterpe
are you my muse
ah to be in the company
of Sappho
in perpetual soulflight
accompanied by a lyre
instead of old habits

7

Who is my muse
who will not allow me
to name her
Tenth muse is it you
painting a hundred tales
from a hundred tribes
in my poems

Looking at Vincent's Trees

in all of nature   expression and soul
Vincent Van Gogh

And in the beginning
the Mama sang a blue-green
song and the invisibles
appeared
then she bronzed a reed
hymned a polyphony of pines
sent up a Chartres of seed
a ninth symphony of fur
a war and peace of feather
and on this Day when you can say
atone-ment or at-one-ment
I call for the name of her muse

Morning walk with Bird Call

It has been months since I've written a blog, because whatever I've had to say the Muse has grabbed for poetry. In fairness to her, she always teases out ideas I haven't thought of.

If I feed her the Muse will work for attention, but her diet, her cravings, can be mysterious. Generally, she feeds on culture, but sometimes I have to make imaginal trips to specialty stores. For example, the prints of the Japanese printmakers Hiroshige and Hokusai are her sushi. She can make a main course out of a complex myth like *The Crane Wife*, or the rain forest. Sometimes it's hot peppers and, on occasion, bitter herbs to remind me of those who are still enslaved.

My curiosity shifts when the Muse is here. I explore images and myth and theater and nature and myself. It's not really research – more like a butterfly collecting nectar, flitting flower to flower. When I find what the Muse wants, she gives me an opening line, or fills me with words.

Where is the Muse when she's not here? On vacation, a religious retreat, maybe having an affair? When she arrives she gives Commandments: *I am your Muse, the Nameless One. Thou shalt have no other interests before Me. Honor My Time and keep it Holy.*

Today she made an appetizer out of a bird call, had a buffet of animals and gave me rhyme and rhythm. I am grateful, and I'll put the new poem here because I want it to be read. And now, after hours of work, I'm starved, so it's time for a late lunch.

Morning Walk with Bird Call

< Life >   < life >   cry the crows
and when I pause
the long-running performance
that plays in my mind
and listen   I am revived
I ask how to keep species alive
and the Muse speaks –
Tell those who don't love
the pawed and tailed
finned and horned
that it's people who need animals
Mention crows and lizards
starfish and ocelots
because profusion startles
the narcissist
Describe lark and lynx and lizard
since feather fur and scale
teach us the genius
of shapeshifting cells
Finally, creatures remind us
that innocence means
not knowing
And we humans know too much
don't we?

The Tree of Blue Leaves

from a medieval painting
by Beatus of Liébana

The tree is painted
  with blue leaves
    a panoply of orange birds
      fill the branches so artfully
All trees call to me
    they are what generates me –
        Apple trees I climbed as a child
        The great African fig where
            100 generations whispered
        The baobab I entered
        And the great Indian banyan
            roots and branch indistinguishable
                sheltering an altar
I am held in this painted tree
  but we are not unchangeable art
  for I change with the seasons
    now I am the red of maples
      slowly browning with age
        leaves not ready to fall
I am a leaf of life's tree
  and I believe in trees
I dreamed I was a druid
    dropped
        into a tree-loss
            of a century
Here what is living
    is in jeopardy
      what is still alive
        is living in me

Anselm Kiefer

Man in Forest

And he brought us to the forest the Black Forest *silva negra*
all you can see in his painting is the dense mass of black trunks
Once his fabled home forest was a hunting ground
fox and beaver and bobcat skinned and auctioned
   Do you know Flaubert's tale of the man
         who couldn't stop killing?
      All that moved   an entire herd
            turned into a pile
               of dead stags
Stag horns are nailed to the front of the museum
in Kiefer's home town a museum of stuffed kill
Growing up by the Danube's source
a hungy artist stalking history
Painting the trunks
over and over   painting himself
in front of the forest
but never animals
never leaves

For the Poet in His Hundredth Year

After Lieut. Lawrence Ferlinghetti was sent to Nagasaki
to survey the damage
  3 square miles of mulch hair and bone
he became a pacifist   *no doubt about it*

How damage can save us   or wound us into wounding
how any flattened landscape may round us
or confound us
demand that we dream of the dead
dread clouds
a shatter of light
  A penny candy store beyond the El is where I first fell
  in love with unreality
he wrote and I believe him
poets do that early
pockets full of jelly beans
lucky charms for when it goes dark
Here is Ferlinghetti in the Paris Review
in uniform   gaunt   unshaven
an officer's peaked cap
staring
And here he is in his straw hat with Allen Ginsberg
smiling into himself
one of the Beats   that beatitude of the almost broken
Oh these sometimes dumbstruck journeys we call lives

Distant Neighbors: Wendell Berry & Gary Snyder

My friend Dan calls from the middle of the country. He has a longish layover in (Minneapolis? Milwaukee? It began with an M) on his way to Europe. He's been reading Charles Wright's poetry and he has a question. Or is it an answer? We have been doing this for decades, learning from the knowledge each of us has of the realms we share.

Every other Wednesday for 40 years Naomi & I meet for dinner and critique our poetry. We dive into the deep of each poem and wrestle with grammar on the surface. We have had similar themes throughout the years, and now, once again, our work has centered – on the Earth. Each of us has written about the other's work, and we've read together. « Each other » becomes an I-and-Thou, a We, united by devotion to our work and love for each other.

Patricia and I share a great love of animals, the wild, the carefully cultivated and we have shared those concerns as they appear in our lives and our work. We are environmentalists, in our own ways and our own words, and we have also read together.

Which brings us to *Distant Neighbors, Selected Letters of Gary Snyder and Wendell Berry*, which focuses on just such a sharing – along with the ideas and insights of two men who will not let their often profound differences damage the love and respect they have for one another. That love and respect was very obvious in their recent reading together.

Wendell Berry is a Christian who refuses the authority of the church, a farmer who admires the tradition of English literature, mentioning Milton and Pope and Blake as his forebears – a man who takes his bible into the forest. Gary Snyder is a Buddhist who admires the Old Ways, hunters and gatherers, and the poetry of China and Japan. For him the authority of Zen comes through a teacher. The way these two men address, resolve and accept their difference is a teaching in itself.

Snyder asked his Sunday school teacher
"Does my dead heifer go to heaven?

No, said the teacher.
Well, I'm not going where my heifer can't go!"
(Reading, June 27)

Berry speaks always of continuity. Continuity between
the wonders of the bible and life in the forest. The spiritual
and the material are not bifurcated – they are one fabric.
(Reading, June 27)

Snyder – "My bible is the archaic universal world body of
folklore and folk mythology." (*Distant Neighbors,* p. 73)

With Snyder in the foothills of the Sierras, and Berry in Port Royal, Kentucky and both men engaged in very public lives as poets and environmentalists, plus family obligations and Berry's farm work, there are few opportunities to get together. But they take the time to write these letters because their love of the land and their commitment to writing creates a duality. They ask each other questions that others might not respond to:

> Berry – What kind of economy would cherish trees?
> (*Distant Neighbors,* p. 124)

In their concern for the environment, and the actions that each took – the books and articles written, the panels they sat on, the conferences they attended, the protests they made, Snyder and Berry are our fore brothers.

And they were prescient, raising issues as though they foresaw the crisis in both government and the environment that we are now living through. In one of the letters Berry writes: "I accept the tragedy that one must take sides." (*Distant Neighbors,* p. 89)

Berry - "Snowden is patriotic. People who make deals know secrets. if a voter enters the booth uninformed – what happens to democracy?" (Reading, June 27)

Snyder, 1980 – "….[there were] conversations with assorted folks after my talk on China, …..where they tried to play down the seriousness of species extinction." (*Distant Neighbors*, p. 69)

They sent letters. By mail. Even after email appeared. Are other writers still writing letters to each other? We email, skype, facebook, tweet, send photos that display what we wish to have known about ourselves and upload the antics of our babies and pets. Shall we have the collected tweets of future artists? The collected FB comments?

Are you familiar with their poetry?

One of my favorite poems – one that I reread over and over – is Berry's *The Peace of Wild Things*, first published in 1968. The poem is written in language a nineteenth century reader would recognize, but the universality and depth of feeling and experience remains as fresh as dawn:

> When despair grows in me
> and I wake in the middle of the night at the least sound
> in fear of what my life and my children's lives may be,
> I go and lie down where the wood drake
> rests in his beauty on the water, and the great heron feeds.
> I come into the peace of wild things
> who do not tax their lives with forethought
> of grief. I come into the presence of still water.
> And I feel above me the day-blind stars
> waiting for their light. For a time
> I rest in the grace of the world, and am free.

(Poemhunter, http://www.poetryfoundation.org/poem/171140)

When did I start reading Gary Snyder? Was the first book *Earth House Hold*? I loved the juxtaposition of Asian literature with the names of plants and animals and the titles of mountains and rivers, the Old Ways of making and being, his sons. The purely experiential, experimental, the sensory and the eternal.

Sustained Yield
> For the treeplanters

Spain, Italy, Albania, Turkey, Greece,
once had hills of
oak and pine

This summer-dry winter-wet
    California
manzanita, valley oak, redwood,
    sugar pine, our folk
sun, air, water,
    our toil,

Topsoil, leafmold, sifted dirt,
hole-in-the-ground

Hold the whip of a tree
steady and roots right
somebody tamp the
    earth, as it's slipped in,
down.

Keep trees growing in this
    Shasta nation alta California
    Turtle Island
ground.
    (*Left Out in the Rain*, p. 134)

This sharing. Of words, of images, of music. How it endows us as humans.

Hosanna

The Mark Morris Dance Company presents
L'Allegro, il Penseroso ed il Moderato

I come to the theater early
carrying Linda Gregg's new book
and just as the house lights dim
I take in   these words –
  "I walk toward the sun
      which is always going down."
and I go in and out of the performance
follow the male lead through
the labyrinth of his steps
then walk down the road with the poet
and when the music brings me back
the sundown wind becomes a violin
and the birds that landed on the road
are a rainbow flight of dancers
and as they lift each other
each one higher than the one before
my arms spontaneously rise
rise in praise

In The Goodness of Time: The Poet and The Great Work

Recently, I read an article about Wallace Stevens in the New Yorker. In it Peter Scheldahl declares that for him the best poem of the 20th century is *The Idea of Order in Key West*.

I re-read the poem after many years, and yes it is beautifully crafted and mythic, about a She and the Sea and it has the power and repetition of waves – but it is a poem written from a metaphysical sky. There is a line in the poem that tells us « She was the single artificer of the world/In which she sang », and I thought the word ‹ he › could be substituted for ‹ she › and it would describe the poet.

Perhaps I responded this way because I'm reading W.S. Merwin's *Moon Before Morning* and the ease and truth and quietness speak to me so sweetly. When he writes of the earth, he is of the earth, and when he writes of the past it is present for him, and when he writes of the Ark you think you can smell the animals.

The Idea of Order in Key West is a peony of a poem, perhaps an entire peony bush – no it has to be larger – the tree of huge red flowers in front of a temple in Laos that I can't identify by name. A tree that blooms year round and holds its canopy up proud as a god.

Merwin has been planting Pritichardia palm trees, native to Hawaii, on his property in Maui for 40 years. His poems are palms, either quietly climbing toward starlight, or they rustle seductively when the wind blows. Or the poems are the small startling flowers of the tropics like the low growing butterfly pea flower – not the brilliant blue variety, but the candid white. I am enamored of the poems particularly because they present the sense of timelessness and presence that one wants age to enable:

Dew Light

Now in the blessed days of more and less
when the news about time is that each day
there is less of it I know none of that
as I walk out through the early garden
only the day and I are here with no
before or after and the dew looks up
without a number or a present age

These 19 acres, 2740 palms, are the work of reclamation the world so badly needs to do – as Thomas Berry describes it in *The Great Work*. The palms, along with bananas and mangos and papaya were planted on land that was damaged first by logging, then pineapple rows were planted vertically so most of the soil washed away. What was left of the soil grew grasses so bitter that an experiment in grazing failed when the cows' lips curled in disgust.

The work of reclamation is what there is when the age of conquering the world is over. Or let us say that reclamation and renewal are the new adventure. What if our own or the world's losses connect us rather than embitter or force us to turn us aside?

Merwin has been aware of what has been happening to our planet for a long time. His great poem *For A Coming Extinction* was published in *The Lice* in 1967, which makes me feel like a Jenny-come-lately to environmental concerns. In 1967 many of us were working and writing against the Vietnam War, and so was he – but he was able to step out of the headlines and into the world to come, which he knew was already there. *For A Coming Extinction* laments:

"Gray whale/ Now that we are sending you to The End/
That great god/ Tell him/ That we who follow you invented
forgiveness/ And forgive nothing."

16

In an interview with Joel Whitney, Merwin talked about the story of Noah:

«I loved that story so much. And I had this fantasy of building an ark in the back yard, because when the rains came, I said, you know, nobody believed Noah. Nobody will believe us either. We can build this boat, but [smirking] where are we going to get the animals?»

Merwin has alternated originality, translation and reclamations since his 30s. I was aware of his long poetic narrative on the history of the Hawaiians, The Folding Cliffs, but I did not know that he had once translated the poetry of the Native American Crow people. In an interview with Edward Hirsch in 1986 Merwin said:

«And I had very much the feeling about the Crow, along with American Indian poetry in general, and many other non-literate poetries, too— that even as we talked about it, it was disappearing. And I think of it as of comparable importance to, say, the burning of the library at Alexandria.»

That comparison. A lessening of scale, a tale of equivalence. Not a diminishing of what we have achieved, but the recognition that others have done as well, and their work is just as significant. This too is the great work.

Transition from Cool to Warm

Anselm Kiefer
Gagosian Gallery NYC

This painter of history   painter of post-war ruin
poisonous myth and the burning of Esther
But when a black spray flares from the artist's self-portrait
a volcano erupts in the empty winter fields he once painted
and the dead heaven on every canvas
is now dawn-warmed or dusk-rayed
The evening of all days the day of all evenings
Then flowered canvases in the next room   wanton with women
A man puts on paint and transmutes into « extasis feminina »
Mouth open always open Who shuts their lips when the goddess requires song?
Vulva open always open Who shuts their lips when the goddess requires longing?
The entire canvas fills with petals and the artist takes possession of desire
You know that's the mystery   the artist taking possession of his she

A Cantata For Paul Klee

I write words on the forehead and round lips.
My faces are truer than life.
Paul Klee

1 As any child knows the sun is always the center of the picture
   it glows canary or gold   this is the only essential color
   all others are the shade play chooses   there are no boundaries
   red grass can bleed into tree   and tree need not be taller than person
   One other rule: the craggy mountains zig-zag across the paper
      and summits come to the point

2 In Klee's Tunisia the town's ornery streets are sun-stilled at sultry noon
   the landscape is melancholy with palms   only the port animates the dreamer
   a coffin   gold leaf and azure is hoisted onto a hearse
   We must be permitted to feel terrors
   Later a cupola the painted moon and a biblical star rise in the sky
      only the artist gardens at night   in the desert's tangible light

3 He lived through all things permitted in the language of tangible form
   an affectionate friend of all familiar objects
   What do we know best?
   Not each other but house   tool   sloop
      the aptitudes of space

4 He was an artist
   a little nearer to the heart of creation than is normal
   Surreptitiously   leaving us
      a fragment of Before

Summoning Ghosts: The Art of Hung Liu

I feel like I'm using my painting as a memorial garden.

I started to write "The theme of Hung Liu's work is..." – when I realized that the word "theme" is totally inadequate. It reminds me of essays for English classes, not the lifelong work of a woman whose goal is the resurrection of the dispossessed.

So many of the peoples of the world experience deprivation and exile. The artist or writer may reinstate them in their old world, describe their suffering, or reshape their identity. It's one part excavation, one part re-creation.

Though she left China and came to study and live in California in 1982, most of Hung Liu's dispossessed are, not surprisingly, Chinese. She researched archives to find photos of those who are not even a footnote to history. Peasant laborers (without the smiles of socialist realism), women soldiers (without the muscles and heroic stance of Maoist art), the poor, the grieving elderly, the 'comfort women' used by Japanese troops during WW II, prostitutes, the exiled, war refugees.

"In terms of true inspiration you need to discover, to excavate, to peel off the layers and try to find out what was there that got lost, for there is always something missing."
   Summoning Ghosts: the Art of Hung Liu, University of California Press, 2012, p. 101

Hung Liu found photos of young prostitutes. Those photos of anonymous teen-age girls were used as advertisements during the end of the last dynasty. She rescues them from obscurity by painting their portraits with great affinity and affection, and lends them a friendly cow, her symbol of humanity, for companionship.

Millions of Chinese were displaced by war and government policy during the twentieth century, and Hung Liu's work focuses, as always, on the human element. I found the painting *By the Rivers of Babylon,* a portrait of an exiled family, particularly moving. I've known the psalm that begins with those words since I was a child:

> "If I forget you, O Jerusalem , let my right hand wither; Let my tongue stick to my palate if I cease to think of you,
> if I do not keep Jerusalem in memory even at my happiest hour."

There are so many Jerusalems! So many who have fled ancestral lands, been forced out of homes.

Hung Liu's work, however painful her choice of subjects, is beautiful and lush. The painted surface is as multi-layered as life itself, and the measured, deliberate dripping of paint adds another dimension, another texture. If you could look closely at *By the Rivers of Babylon*, you would see that the children are eating from colorful Ming dynasty bowls!

That imaginal juxtaposition appears in so many of her paintings. A young girl, bent over with heavy burdens, is surrounded by doves, fantastic bird wings, and painted Buddhas. Cranes and blossoms and butterflies surround whores and wounded warriors. It is not prettifying, but a loving adornment of the dispossessed. She holds the opposites: the heron in elegant plumage or the inevitable blossoms of Chinese art – juxtaposed with poverty and displacement.

I was so moved by a series of simple paintings. I wish I had photos for you. Each day the artist painted some object in her mother's home during the 49 days of mourning after the elderly woman's death. She painted useful objects, like the kitchen tools her mother used every day, each object made eloquent. Hung Liu is a woman who understands the need for ceremony, but she invents rituals for her own soul's particular journey.

And then come the paintings of a flame, one after another. The spirit kept alive. The soul guided by light on its journey. An ancient impulse to light a candle to accompany grief. One painting, one candle, after another.

Autumn-Woven Runes

A winter-barren painting is Anselm Kiefer's homage to Paul Celan
a line of the poet's hope-spurned German is strung
across the top of the canvas like a clothesline
just the soul drying in the cold light
      Des Herbstes Runengespint
        "autumn
            that which has been woven
                runes"
I turn the pages of Celan's Selected   Collected   Last
skimming poems for autumn   woven   runes
until   stirred   the poems thicken in me
I quicken to *no hand holds me   no hand to hold you*
back   no hand to take you forward
suspended   unreachable in the corner of time
while   outside   a leaf the brown of November   spins
though there is no wind   stem-trapped   in a spiderless web

Another Kiefer painting:
   A branch grows out of a man's heart
      the artist as Gilgamesh holds a flaming branch in the forest
        Is it his source of light   or will he torch the woods?
          Have other plants spontaneously
            burst into flame
              besides the Burning Bush?

Note:
Anselm Kiefer   Contemporary German artist
Paul Celan (1920-1970)

23

Metamorph ising

for the artist Kiki Smith

Metamorphosis means more than once
as it is with egg larva pupa butterfly
as it is with some lives when larval stripes
and slow ripple are shed again and again
then comes the mimicry of dead leaf
till finally crysalis splits and out flutters
wet-winged splendor
I saw a woman born of a doe
I saw a woman step out
of the body of a wolf
There is return
Gaia I know you are wounded
it is hard for you to breathe
I dreamed you shed your scarred
stripmined surface
and underneath was skin
the pink of healing
Now you must rest
and all of us   wolf doe
woman man become pupa
In our silk cocoons
we wait
suspended

Would It Not Represent a Minotaur?

Picasso. Revisited. An exhibit at the De Young. Another exhibit at SFMOMA features his work. Jerome Rothenberg & Pierre Joris have edited and translated his journals into poems. (Pablo Picasso: The Burial of the Count of Orgaz & other poems, Exact Change, 2004). "Poetry Unhinged" Michel Leiris calls it in his Afterword, "closer to Dadaist nihilism than to surrealism." Was that Picasso's desire, to destroy meaning? We know how he broke from the past, but nihilism? I won't continue without giving you a sample, and I'll choose at random:

> the slender sojourn of the secret price of pain simmers on the
> low fire of memory where the onion plays the star it
> detaches itself from its lines having read and reread the past
> but at the crack of the riding-whip caught straight in the eyes
> (p. 98)

"the secret price of pain simmers on the low fire of memory" is a wonderful image, but my brain, which looks for continuity, for meaning, for revelation or narrative, gives up, as though I have entered a dense labyrinth with no center, no way in – but there is always a hint of minotaur, for he wrote during the same period

> "If all the roads I have been down were marked on a map and
> joined up with a line, would it not represent a Minotaur?"
> (*Picasso: Masterpieces from the Musee National Picasso*, Paris
> Fine Arts Museums of San Francisco. p. 141)

The minotaur, half bull/half man, at the center of the labyrinth, the garden. What, I ask myself, if there was no censor, no conscious linear narrative, between oneself and the maze of images, feelings, and archetypes that make up what is usually hidden, would that explain the fecundity and astonishing flow of his imagery?

25

Another random selection:

> entangled in the rainbow of their feather oxen plowing up the
> flames of crystal of the howling that perfumes the angles and
> the curves snared by the web of nails and begging help   (p. 206)

The selection covers a page, and these pages were written daily – a kaleidoscope, a display of fireworks, or simply an inventory, or what comes in with the tide. Imagine a basin that is never empty, but the source is unknown.

Years ago I concentrated on Picasso's experience during the war years in order to understand the relationship between art and terror, which is so strong in the 20th century. The 'macho', the womanizer accused of sadism, of feelings of omnipotence, the toreador lover, and endless innovator experienced terror during the Spanish Civil and World War II, a terror he was ashamed of. Here is a selection from his journal:

"....sky....fear and anguish...what horror what distress and what cold in the bones and what unpleasant odor ....wing.... ...desperate cry... girl dead of fear....black liquid [rains]...the dead fall drop by drop.... clouds shit...horror and despair....wing[ed tank stuck in the blue sky... the nest of vipers...the desperate cries of birds...the infinite center of void on the skin torn off the house....
  (*Picasso and the War Years: 1937-1945*, Ed Steven A. Nash,
  Thames and Hudson, 1998, p. 57))

The savagery of the war resulted in paintings of literal butchery: The skull of a sheep and a rack of butchered lamb are alone in one of Picasso's paintings.

The Spanish painter Zubaran painted racks of lamb, and the skull was a frequent subject of Spanish and medieval painting in general, as a symbol of vanity or the brevity of life. But Picasso's skulls still had their meat on them. His overburdened psyche found release in art, and despite the

Occupation, and the warnings and threats he received, he continued to paint what he felt.

In 1942 the wartide was turning. America had entered the war, the allies had invaded North Africa, and the Nazis were facing defeat in Russia. Picasso began the drawing for Man with a Lamb, and you probably have seen the result, the bronze which currently is on exhibit at the De Young. A young man stands before us holding a large lamb.

Lamb of God? Good Shepherd? Abraham's sacrifice? Picasso would only say "there's nothing religious about it at all. There's no symbolism in it" and that he just wanted "a human feeling, a feeling that has always existed." (Ibid, p. 112)

The sculpture remained in his studio for the rest of the war, and if postwar visitors wanted a photo, Picasso posed next to the sculpture. I think this was a victory – over the panic-stricken, butchered imagery that had taken him over, and he took pride in this victory. He had overcome hell and returned to the simple humanity of everyday life. "Dadaist nihilism"? I don't think so. The urge to annihilate, in the man, in the world, was overcome.

At least in that instance. In that world. At that time.

Picasso's Portrait of a Woman Weeping

That ridiculous hat
her face made up in
prisms of comic book color
those petrified animal eyes
The face of Europe
breaking and weeping

The woman   Dora Maar
the cruel brushstrokes of her lover
her crystalline surface   shattered
What man
can watch a woman weeping
without seeing his own death?

Frida Kahlo Who Is Still With Me

I drank to drown my sorrows,
but the damned things learnt how to swim.

Frida's blue house that I find in San Angel 1963
a house full of ceramic skulls
    with her Frog who she kissed
      and it became a bigger frog
Frida in the short film haunted by Villa Lobos
    in the glamor of winged eyebrows
      in flamboyant Tehauana ruffles
The artist painting herself bleeding
    in Henry Ford Hospital
        painting herself in a steel corset
        teaching us how
           to transmute
             pain
Frida & Tequila
    & Trotsky
      & the People
Painting her celebrity
    instead of her pain
    and the skull
      who chased her
      throughout
      her life

For the Artist Pedro Friedeberg

Take me into your world
which you made for me
Yes I'm sure it was made for me
Your surreal renderings of
an imaginary Renaissance
A menorah of hands
An arm ending in toes
many-handed swirl
of a woman in gold
I don't seem to mind
that you leave out nature
since green already rides in my pocket
When did you think I would figure out
that you led me into a labyrinth?
But this is Mexico
and the bull in the maze
is no minotaur

Let the Animals

for the artist Diana Friedeberg

I saw fire burn in the mouth of a lion
I don't know if she eats flame
or the blaze flares from her hunger

You will find the lion in the curio cabinet of the psyche
next to a glass jaguar with a clock face inside its body
Time is running out

This curio cabinet has a collection of shells
no beachcomber will ever find
I too want to spiral poetry around a conch shell
your eyes following every word

The curious Victorians
learned that eyes looked out at them from everywhere
    all those butterflies pinned to velvet
    those drawers and drawers of labeled beetles
Even the fusty stuffed furniture knew their every move

Outside the curio cabinet it is no less miraculous
the immobile eye of the owl
six-sided lens of the butterfly
square eyes of the goat
who can almost see behind her body
Let the animals turn the pages
of the book of life
since we know so little
about how light enters the body
how heat radiates
from within

The Cave Painter

When we stayed in the Lot Valley in southern France, we visited the cave called Pech-Merle, and saw the hand prints, and the powerful images of dotted horses, bison and mammoths. *They've invented everything!* Picasso said when he visited Lascaux.

Lascaux was closed to the public when all the human exhalations caused mold to form on the art. Chauvet, discovered in 1994, had art older than all the others. To protect the art, a steel door had been placed on the narrow entrance, and only a small team of experts would be allowed to enter. One of those experts came to Cal with slides shortly after the discovery, and the auditorium was filled. My friend Tim and I stood in back to hear him speak. The images of cave art he showed were startling masterpieces, and we thought we would only ever see these images in books or slides.

I read all I could on Chauvet, intrigued by this mysterious 30,000 year old art whose origins and meaning might never be understood. Was it Tim who gave me *The Mind in the Cave*, by David Lewis-Williams, that remarkable book that claimed shamanism and initiation as the basis of paleolithic art? There was, Lewis-Williams claimed, a direct tie between the shamanic rock art of Australia and the ancient images on the cave walls.

In Lewis-Williams' earlier book, *The Signs of All Times*, written with the anthropologist T. A. Dowson:

> "The authors cited laboratory experiments with subjects in an induced trance state which suggested that the human optic system generates the same types of visual illusions, in the same three stages, differing only slightly by culture, whatever the stimulus: drugs, music, pain, fasting, repetitive movements,

solitude, or high carbon-dioxide levels (a phenomenon that is common in close underground chambers). In the first stage, a subject sees a pattern of points, grids, zigzags and other abstract forms (familiar from the caves); in the second stage, these forms morph into objects—the zigzags for example, might become a serpent. In the third and deepest stage, a subject feels sucked into a dark vortex that generates intense hallucinations, often of monsters or animals and feels his body and spirit merging with theirs." [Or maybe the spirits are contacted?]

http://www.newyorker.com/reporting/2008/06/23/080623fa_fact_thurman#ixzz1NidPi4EF

When we first read about Werner Herzog's 3D film *The Cave of Forgotten Dreams*, we were very excited, and last night, when my back was sufficiently healed to sit in a theater seat for the length of a film, we went to see it. Constant background music, eerily contemporary, kept us from experiencing the deep ancient silence of the cave, but the images on the curved and sometimes undulating surfaces were remarkable. Just a few lines, just a few perfectly executed outlines, (what Zen artists once strived for), and the animals of Aurignacian Europe, as though drawn yesterday, emerged from the rock face. Were they spirit animals coming through the porous rock from the underworld they inhabited? Rhinoceros, lions, leopard, bison, aurochs and horses – a quartet of horse heads so beautifully drawn one thinks of Renaissance draughtsmen.

Herzog says it is as though the human soul awakened here. On a phallus-shaped pinnacle suspended from the cave ceiling is the only picture of the human figure. It shows a bison above and surrounding a woman's sex. A fused figure, from a shamanic vision, perhaps. There is a bison-woman at Pech-Merle as well.

Recently we downloaded a film made by and about the Inuit people, *The Journals of Knud Rasmussen*. (http://www.isuma.tv/fastrunnertrilogy) At the end of the film a shaman must either give up the old religion or starve. He sends his spirits, who have always been with him, away. He tells them they must go, and they are sobbing, they are weeping and holding on to each other, and they finally walk away. They turn around after walking a few yards and look back, but the shaman repeats that now he must accept Jesus or starve, because that is the condition of the Christian feast another converted Inuit is holding nearby. He must eat the taboo animal organs that shamans must never touch. That will be his communion. He is crying. He is without choice. He has a wife and daughter and followers to feed, and he does not want to die the agony of starvation.

I think of the shamans of the Aurignacian, and the power of their visions. An archaeologist in Herzog's film says that perhaps Homo Sapiens is the wrong name for us. Perhaps we should be known as Homo Spiritualis.

The Cave Painter

And then
  suddenly
      to us it is sudden
        but not to them
     they discovered murder

the animals had been idolized terrors
but now they had the spear
when they woke up to what they were doing
it was not morning
killing came into their nightly seance
animal spirits invaded their dreams
carrying spears thicker and taller than cedars
and shredded carcasses
     washed down night's river

and the dreamers were us
just as smart and no longer innocent
and they promised   they begged   they offered
and they couldn't forget
and they made it the task of one man   one woman
to remember   to be remembering every minute
and he or she   make it she
went into the caves on hands and knees   snake belly crawl
touched her hand to the farthest wall
she knew   they all knew by now
   they were certain
     the spirits lived on the other side

Let her place the torch on the bear-trodden floor
and press her hands against the shivery membrane –
She   the one with hands   the one with a body

cont'd

the gods count on our hands   they use our bodies
the animal spirits see the future through cro magnon eyes
see the hills   the rivers   the forest   there were animals **yes**
    but not them   not a one

so they send her their own true shape
       and she grinds her colors   picks up charcoal
         and leaves us the auroch   the bison

Enter the caves
     and the ancient age
  of what you believe
       we just invented
      will be shown to you

     and you will not be afraid

About the Author

Leah Shelleda is Professor Emerita of Humanities and Philosophy at the College of Marin. Her poems have appeared in many journals and anthologies. Her chapbook, *A Flash of Angel*, won the Blue Light Press prize, and *Adorning the River* won the Red Berry Press chapbook prize. Her book of poetry is entitled *After the Jug Was Broken*, and her anthology, *The Book of Now: Poetry for the Rising Tide* includes herself and six other women poets speaking to the current state of our world.

Leah has been a weaver of wall hangings as well as words, an ardent gardener, life-long seeker, social activist, and a crone-in-training. She is happily embedded in a large family, including eight grandchildren and a great-nephew.

www.ingramcontent.com/pod-product-compliance
Lightning Source LLC
Chambersburg PA
CBHW022348040426
42449CB00006B/772